NICK THO

trical engineer in the Royal Air Force, serving as an officer for 16 years, and later worked in data communications for Nortel. He was General Secretary of the Anthroposophical Society in Great Britain for 21 years, and researched the practical application of projective geometry with colleagues Lawrence Edwards and John Wilkes. His major research interest is the development and application of Steiner's discovery of negative space, with the aim of building a bridge between conventional and spiritual science. He lectures widely on this and other subjects, and is the author of *Science Between Space and Counterspace* and *Space and Counterspace*.

FREEDOM THROUGH LOVE

The Search for Meaning in Life
Rudolf Steiner's Philosophy of Freedom

Nick Thomas

TEMPLE LODGE

Temple Lodge Publishing
Hillside House, The Square
Forest Row, RH18 5ES

www.templelodge.com

Published by Temple Lodge 2014

A catalogue record for this book is available from the British Library

ISBN 978 1 906999 57 5

Cover by Andrew Morgan Design
Typeset by DP Photosetting, Neath, West Glamorgan
Printed and bound by Berforts Ltd., Herts.

Contents

What is it to be human? What is knowledge? Philosophy tries to solve the problems of whether we can know anything for certain, and whether we are free. Clearly the concept of freedom lives amongst us. Where might it come from if freedom does not exist? In a world of moral dilemmas and increasing emancipation from old standards based on religion and authority, what matters most? Rarefied philosophical arguments about abstract ideas? Surviving from day to day? Reliance on the authority of science or some religion? Surely the richness and problems of our relationships with other people are the most pressing and 'real' aspects of our life! No philosophical denial of their reality can remove them; for example, to point out that we do not know what reality is or that all our supposed knowledge is illusion does nothing to alleviate the problems we have to contend with every day. The unreasonable and harsh boss, the car that won't start just when I need it, the shame at something I have done, the trepidation at having to perform in a new situation, coping with illness and bereavement and so on are what Whitehead[1] would

1

call 'stubborn irreducible facts' immune to mere intel-
lectualising.

Yet most if not all people seek for meaning in their
lives. Am I really merely a speck on an undistinguished
planet accidentally placed in a solar system which is part
of one of millions of galaxies in a vast clockwork universe? Or does it matter that I try to realize ideals, relate
to other people constructively and even lovingly fulfil
my obligations, try to understand what I am in reality?
Why do I suffer pangs of conscience? What makes some
people risk their lives for others in deeds of courage?
Why does music move me so deeply? To dismiss life as
worthless, meaningless or merely the play of chance is to
give up on the deeper questions of life.

The following exploration of these questions is based
on Rudolf Steiner's philosophy[2], but from a different
starting point to suit modern times, with liberal inter-
pretations and additions.

So where do I start in a modern setting? I will accept
as fact that people seek meaning, and must reckon with
what for them are pressing realities of everyday life.
Then I will trace that back to the kind of answer
traditional philosophy might value. Let us not start with
abstract questions far from life, but from life itself! That
requires above all that I start with people and their
relationships, for there lie the most pressing questions.
Of course that is to start with what is most difficult, but
at least it starts from where we are.

My inner life of feeling approaches most closely the questions I have about life. Why am I concerned about a person? Because I feel for him or her. 'Concern' is an informed feeling, not merely an abstract thought. Why don't I like being ill? Because I don't like the discomfort that goes with it, or I feel the fear of death. To value something involves feeling. If I am insulted or praised, I respond out of feeling, but of course also with the help of thinking. No response would seem necessary if it evoked no feeling in me. To appreciate art involves an aesthetic awareness which is a more subtle aspect of feeling. This leads towards the kind of feeling that discerns meaning, for meaning as intended at this stage is more than a mere definition. Most important of course is love, but in a moment I must come to an agreement as to what I mean by that word.

It is clear that 'feeling' is not a simple term, and I do not intend it be anything like an axiom or self-evident starting point in a formal sense, but straightforwardly an experience known to us all at some level. It *is* a starting point in the sense that it starts from where we are, and for most is a stubborn, undeniable aspect of our existence. Some people are foolish enough to suppose that feeling should be suppressed or denied, thereby throwing away much of the richness of life. It happens to us just as the impressions of our senses happen to us, and it would be no more stupid to say that all sense experiences should be suppressed or denied. Sense perceptions contrast with what happens when we think about our experiences, for then we seek to understand them and arrive at ideas, categories and concepts. Feeling is a form of perception when viewed from this perspective, and suffers from all the same objections as are levelled against other sense experiences, so we must aim to deal with those objections in due course. What must be emphasized at this stage is that feeling and sense perceptions are experiences of importance to us, no matter what their philosophical status may turn out to be. Will you love your mother less, or enjoy a good meal less because someone tells you those experiences may be illusions? Yet seekers of knowledge would like to know how to assess their experiences. Are my joys and sufferings like yours? Are they part of the world or merely a subjective impression? If I see a ghost, is it an illusion to be disregarded or is it real on some level? If I have a foreboding that the aircraft I am about to board will crash, should I take it seriously? Are those thinkers correct who think that we, along with our experiences and thoughts, are merely part of a computer simulation being conducted by a higher intelligence? Was George (Bishop) Berkeley[3] right in supposing we are thought by God? Are naive realists correct who regard all sense-based experiences to be real? Or are the sceptics right who think we cannot know anything for certain? Regardless of these possibilities, for that is all they are, we will proceed on the basis that for whatever reason we do have perceptions and experience feelings, along with the accompanying thought activity, and must go from there. I am not assuming that either perception or thinking is merely some kind of brain activity, for that is an unproved theory. I am accepting at the outset that they are for me facts of my existence, the status of which I seek to understand.

There are many kinds of experience that can evoke feelings. If someone kicks your shin you will feel sharp pain. This is perhaps the first level, along with other feelings arising from bodily disorders or indeed pleasures arising from the body. Such a feeling is a perception of the state of my body. Then I find I like some things and dislike others, which are more inward feelings, especially when not merely reactions to sensations such as taste or smell. I may feel satisfaction with what I have just done, or of course the reverse. This is not a perception of the body, but an example of another level of perception about my situation. Or I may look at a painting and experience it artistically, which is an aesthetic feeling reaching out beyond myself. Again it is a perception, in this case of my relation to the painting, of a kind distinct from the above two examples. Or I may experience my relationship to another person, perhaps as contempt, respect, pity or love for example. I perceive my relationship to the other person through that feeling. In all these examples feeling can be seen as a perception of myself, from the merely bodily up to the perception of my relationship to others.

When I refer to love I mean more than mere sexual experience. I can love a picture or an idea without any sexual connotation, and I can also love a person in the platonic sense. That love and sex may go together merely emphasizes that the love is a distinct experience or perception from the sexual aspect. I started from feeling and have indicated that it is a form of perception, in order to lead to that kind of feeling called love. For I wish to show that a philosophy of life must be based on love. What is important for me is, ultimately, what I love. Everybody needs love, even if only the love of money! Something has meaning for me if love is involved. That proposal must of course be examined (see Annex B), but it seems pretty clearly to be the case, although the converse should not be construed. As shown there, even the meaning of a statement involves feeling. In the last 30 years meaning has again become a serious subject of philosophical discussion, especially what is meant by the meaning of life.

What of people who act out of hatred? Consider for example animal rights activists who are willing to injure human beings for their cause, or terrorists likewise. I assume that such an activist started out from a love of animals, but that love turned into a hatred of those who misuse animals. Acting out of hatred is not the same as acting out of love for animals. Much fanaticism can be understood in this light: an initial love of something ends up as a hatred of its opposite. However even that cannot necessarily explain plain evil, where even love may never have been involved. But the salient point is precisely that love was never involved.

There are, however, different kinds of love. We all have the ability to think, we (mostly) have feelings, and we are capable of exerting our will when we take action (or refrain from a temptation!). Consider feeling first: empathy for others is an example of love in the realm of feeling. If my feeling is devoid of love I am unlikely to help others or understand their situation. Regarding will, what enables a person to act courageously? Is not courage love in the realm of the will? Why else would people risk themselves in such acts? Finally there is also love in the realm of thinking. The most obvious manifestation is enthusiasm for an idea or a thought. Why do I trouble myself to try and understand the world, its laws, its history, its people? Surely because there is love in my thinking! As a counter-example, for most of us the necessity to take the trouble to complete our tax return is met with antipathy. There seems to be no love in our thinking there—not to mention the plethora of forms and procedures that plague the lives of those trying to be active in education, care of the disadvantaged, care of the elderly and so on.

Does every soldier who plunges into battle act out of

love in the will? He may well if genuinely espousing the cause for which he fights, or if he loves duty, but again he may be a driven conscript. In that case he plunges into battle out of fear of the consequences of not doing so, which is a case of displaced love for he prefers the hope he will survive to the certainty of punishment and disgrace or even summary execution. But that does not deny that real courage is love in the will. I do not wish to devalue what so many suffered in world wars, but rather to honour them.

Is every charitable act based on love in the realm of feeling? Perhaps not, for it is proverbial that charity may be cold, in which case the deed is based on some other kind of love, e.g. of the prestige arising from demonstrable acts of 'good'. Unfortunately much hypocrisy lives here, but that does not devalue the genuine cases where love lives in the feelings that lead to action. Indeed it is just that which distinguishes between the genuine and the hypocritical.

There is always the danger of cynicism, where every noble deed is devalued to disguised selfishness. This is even fuelled by Darwinism, which perforce bases itself on selfish survival instincts and, in sociobiology, is driven to almost comic prevarications to explain away altruism in the animal kingdom. Let the cynic ask himself what fruit he wins from it. In this essay I dismiss this attitude in the face of the overwhelming evidence for positive human acts of goodness and love, which are only underlined by their opposite, illustrating the importance of love or the lack of it.

Is idealism always positive? I ask this question because it has been seen also to be destructive. What is an ideal, if not my love for an idea? Some love the idea of social justice, some of the creative power of individual initiative, some of human freedom, some of health and so on. When these ideals remain positive and lead to constructive acts surely we witness the higher aspects of humanity. To love an idea is a uniquely human possibility, quite distinct from instinctive altruism in animals. Science regards human beings as no more than animals, but that is an unproved theory undermined by the inner life of human beings that it cannot deal with. I illustrated destructive idealism earlier in the case of fanatical animal activists who act out of hate instead of love. For they cannot act purely out of love if they are willing to injure human beings for their cause. We witness today other examples in fanatical approaches to racism and sexism. To love the differences between peoples that leads to the richness of humanity is in complete contrast to the hatred expressed in racial discrimination. Here a one-sided love of a particular racial type can lead to the hatred of other types. It should be clear that a sentimental idea of 'gushing' love is not intended here; courage as love in the will is the best counter to such a possibility.

One of the most interesting and important ideals is that of human freedom. It is a fact that it exists as an ideal and many have died for it. So it is mere blindness to dismiss freedom summarily in the face of that fact. However science seems to show that human freedom is an illusion, especially as a result of the work of Benjamin Libet (see Annex A). For now I note the fact that the ideal of freedom patently exists. Intimately connected with that is the fact that 'love' is not a scientific idea, so no proper scientific experiment can say anything about it. 'How do you define it?' I was once asked. It is not a matter of definition but of fact. I know it exists because I have experienced it. If you have not, I am sorry for you. It is clear that if human beings are complex machines subject only to the law of physical cause and effect, freedom is an illusion. But, that thesis is completely unproved because the unscientific idea of love is an essential part of much human action. Science needs widening to embrace inwardness in human experience before it is qualified to pontificate on human action, not to mention religion and other spiritual topics.

Accepting the existence and power of love, it is clear that love cannot be compelled. I cannot compel you to love me, and I cannot be compelled to love a person or an idea. Equally I cannot find love without insight. Love shares with other feelings the fact that it is a form of perception. In the loved one I perceive that with which I can unite and go beyond myself. Indeed love tends to replace my concern for myself with concern for the loved one. Here is the bedrock of freedom, just because

10

love cannot be compelled. Love is the ultimate basis of freedom. A free deed involves the different kinds of love outlined above.

First I must have an idea for what needs to be done; love in thinking embraces a need in the world crying out to be met. This is quite easy really, for who cannot understand the need for equal rights, social justice and so on? The difficulty arises in grasping the right idea in an individual and novel situation where general laws are unhelpful. Fresh and creative ideas are then needed, and the interest to seek such ideas.

Secondly I need to turn the above insight into a plan of action, which requires imagination for I need to form some kind of picture or plan of what can be done. Usually this is much harder than grasping an idea, as is usually the case in passing from the general to the specific. Love in the realm of feeling is needed to perceive how I am related to the situation in such a way as to arrive at a picture of what I can do (as opposed to what 'someone else should do').

Thirdly I need love in the realm of will, to have the courage to go ahead and act in a novel and untested situation. An important aspect of this is love of the circumstances and environment into which action may take place. Does my intuition and imagination really belong there, or will it disturb the *status quo* in a damaging way? Am I engaged on an ego-trip, or is my plan truly creative and valuable?

Notice that positive action is envisaged here. It is easy to say 'do not' e.g., do not kill. What is required is quite clear. But to say 'love thy neighbour' involves understanding the individual needs of my neighbour and his character including his pride, independence, prejudices and so on. A truly free deed is a creative one because usually something quite new is required of me.

In contrast to the above the enemies of freedom are potted thinking, convention in feeling and routine in the will. What is the tried and tested action, or what did so-and-so do last time? What is the accepted approach in such a case? What do other people think of this? These three are the enemies of initiative, for true freedom lies in the *ability to take initiative*, which in turn is the exercise of love in the three spheres concerned. The boring discussion of 'freedom of choice' is a very minimal case of freedom, for it implies the choices are already pre-determined, reducing the possibility of initiative to a minimum. That is not to say that previous experience must be ignored, or the insights of great thinkers should be set aside. The point is to act out of insight, not mere imitation. Some people never have an original idea in their lives, and are then well advised to study the ideas of others. Others are unimaginative and must seek help in forming a plan of action, while still others are blind to the true state of the world they live in and need asistance in assessing the value of a plan of action. To system-atically disagree with authority is as unfree as slavishly following it. To find love for other people's ideas, moral tenets and techniques is most valuable, for then new ideas and actions are part of a greater context. That involves an interest in others that informs initiative rather than stifling it. Greater insight may then be achieved rather than a narrow self-interest.

Of course it is scarcely to be expected that we can act in this ideal manner all the time. Many actions in practical life are unfree as we are constrained by circumstances and by other people as well as by our own limitations. What is important is to grasp the possibility of free action in the above sense, and then learn gradually to apply it. If that possibility is denied then freedom is banished, for unloved constraint can always be traced back to causes external to the individual. Furthermore, when confronted by necessities we can seek insight into why we are subject to them and come to love also the world we live in and its requirements. Philosophers who, in seeking freedom, ended up in a tragic vacuum simply missed the role of love in freedom. Rudolf Steiner remarked in a lecture that freedom is not something to be proved, but to be taken hold of![4]

Surely, it may be objected, I am compelled by love? I feel I must serve the interests of the one I love and so am unfree. This is an example either of never having experienced love or else mere intellectualizing. The intellect cannot value anything, for that is not its role. It can understand, but to value requires feeling. The

13

opposite to the above objection is in reality true, for the greatest unfreedom is experienced if I am prevented from carrying out my initiative or am unable to help the one I love. Free action does not exist in a vacuum, and the more I value the world and all beings in it the more my love for action becomes significant and creative. Knowledge is obviously of great importance if an action is to be free. This was anticipated in the third step involved in a free deed, where knowledge of the circumstances in which I will act is important.

It will be observed that the above approach is entirely individual, and does not relate to the actions of groups, nations or organizations. The greatest unfreedom can often be observed in group action, where the individual tends to be suppressed in favour of group slogans and norms. The three spectres of potted thinking, convention and routine readily arise where groups are on the move. Of course there can be groups with high ideals, but they usually require much of their members, who in turn bear love for the ideals of the group within themselves and thus are committed to the group out of freedom rather than compulsion. However, in this essay it is individual freedom that is of primary concern, for only individuals can be free.

Two possible objections may seem relevant: it all seems too 'nice', and mere licence may be confused with freedom. Taking the latter first, the opportunity to submit to sexual urges, overeating and drinking and so on simply does not measure up. Far from being free in the above sense, such actions are compelled by the body, even if that compulsion is surrendered to joyfully. The distinction between eating because I love life and must needs eat, and eating for its own sake is patently obvious, and so it is in other cases. But, if I act out of love for myself, does that not meet my criteria for a free deed? It clearly may do so, but there is one essential proviso. If, as is suggested, a free deed is entirely based on love, then a deed based on love for myself must not involve lack of love for others or the world. Unfortunately many acts based on self-love are detrimental to others. For example the action of criminals falls squarely under this heading, as does seduction with no intention of long-term commitment, as does gaining advantages at the expense of others. Which of us is innocent in that respect? As Hamlet pessimistically pointed out: 'Use every man after his desert, and who should 'scape whipping?'

Is it all too 'nice'? Anyone can say 'love, love, love' without appreciating what genuine love entails. I knew a woman whose husband suffered from Alzheimer's disease already in his forties; he suffered gradual but remorseless deterioration for ten long years. Her love for him never wavered despite her being blamed by him and his family for his woes, as well as having to contend with his three suicide attempts, and yet hold together a home for her two children. When love is tested, if true it may be far from sentimental and 'nice'. Those who 'lay down their life for others', i.e. do so out of love rather than compulsion, further illustrate the point. Think of Captain 'Titus' Oates who was suffering from severe frostbite on Scott's Antarctic expedition; knowing he was holding back his companions he walked out into the freezing conditions never to be seen again. Free deeds can be joyful but they can also, and very often are, severely testing. The view espoused here can cut to the quick.

I have so far concentrated on the immediacy of action based on love in a common-sense fashion, and deliberately non-scientifically. The reason for the latter is not out of contempt for science, but because science sets its limits and agenda so as to exclude phenomena like love and inner experience. For all the success of the scientific method and its achievements, on the one hand it needs extending to include inward experience, and on the other there is no prima facie reason why all matters of importance need be solved scientifically, e.g. religion. But modern people do generally act rationally and like to base their decisions on reason rather than authority. For example, if the washing machine breaks down you could pray to God to fix it, call in a witch doctor to remove the spell or get a mechanic who understands washing machines to repair it. I leave the choice to you!

Levels of Freedom

How many times have you heard of (or had!) a great idea that never gets off the launching pad? There are two components of an action: on the one hand an idea and on the other the drive to actually do something about it. It has been said that people of a choleric disposition go looking for trouble, and if they can't find it they make it. Some people like action for its own sake, and given an idea will take off vertically to do something about it. Others dream great and noble dreams but have no impulse to realize them practically. The motive for an action is composed of both aspects, i.e. both an idea and the drive to carry it out. When the police seek a suspect for a crime, they look for a likely motive that may give them a lead. The motive can be an idea but usually involves some drive to act such as hatred, revenge or the desire for money.

Ideas range from those prompted by egoism to those based purely on unselfish love. In between ideas for action may be derived from authority or programmes. An authority may be religion, science, the state, a dominating friend or partner, and so on, while a programme may be animal rights, equality of the sexes, eradication of racism, protection of the environment or a political aim, to name just a few. The more an idea coming from such sources is not based on insight and love the less is it free. A truly free motive requires the idea to be based on love in thinking. It can of course come from religion, say, but be based on insight rather than compulsion.

Driving forces to act range from instinct to unselfish love in the will. In between may lie tact, feeling and practical experience. The roof of the house is leaking, and practical experience dictates action sooner rather than later to avoid a worsening situation. A feeling of compassion may cause me to act, a desire to seek its gratification. The point is that these elements of my life drive me to action. The highest level of drive is free from external pricks and is based on my own inner decision to take action, which requires love in the will. It is necessary to emphasize that all of these intermediate 'levels', and others, are not to be dismissed because they are not fully free. I duck instinctively when someone throws a missile at me, and am pleased I have done so! I would actually feel unfree if prevented from mending the leak in the roof.

Practical life involves actions based on motives that are a varied mix of these possible ideas and drives, as is obvious. I have the idea that I must go to work to support my family, and am driven to do so by practical experience. I understand a difficulty that besets a friend and am driven by my feeling of compassion to help her.

The various combinations of idea and drive make up the motives of my life of action. How they combine, and with what strength, depends upon my character. The point is that they are rarely completely free, but on the other hand they seem necessary. A fully free deed in the sense of this essay is one where love in thinking derives an idea for action, and love in the will leads to its realization. External inducements are at a minimum, or are absent. What is being contended is that *fully free deeds are possible*. Difficult they may be, but freedom is not an illusion; its possibility is part of us and may be taken hold of the more we come to experience and act out of love. Such a deed assumes I am capable of having insight and have some understanding of the world I live in.

The Role of the Senses

A philosopher will probably object that I have accepted the existence of feelings and love and much else naive-realistically, i.e. without proper examination. Agreed. That issue must now be examined. If sense perceptions are illusory, for example, so perhaps are my feelings? Then freedom could vanish in a puff of philosophical smoke, to be replaced by bodily-compelled actions. I need some solid ground to stand on inwardly in order to turn what has been said about freedom into secure knowledge.

As indicated earlier, feelings are a species of perception. I am aware of my environment through sense perceptions such as colours, tastes, sounds, and so on, but aware of myself through feeling. I only turn perceptions to useful account by thinking about them and forming concepts. Taking a patch of yellow as an example of a sense perception, several questions arise. Is the yellow part of the object where I see it, or is it some kind of illusion conjured up by my brain? Is the yellow I see the same as what you see? How could I test that? First of all it is important to distinguish my direct experience of the yellow from the scientific description of the radiation entering my eye, which is supposed to explain the colour.

Galileo[5] divided the realm of qualities into so-called *primary qualities*, which are measurable and shareable, and *secondary qualities*, which are supposedly subjective and not amenable to scientific investigation (also Thomas Hobbes[6] by implication). Thus the weight of a brick, the length of a rod, the volume of the Earth and the magnitude of the force of gravity acting on me are examples of primary qualities, which independent observers may measure and compare. Science is then possible. But my experience of a patch of yellow, of the sound of middle-C played on a violin, of the taste of an apple, of my feeling of enjoyment when I eat the apple, are examples of secondary qualities. In daily life all my experience comes to me in the form of secondary qualities, whereas primary qualities are derived from them by special experimental arrangements which themselves are based on secondary qualities. Twentieth-century dogma regarded secondary qualities as being merely subjective and outside the realm of science. Since all primary qualities rest on them, however, those very primary qualities are no more reliable than what supports them. A house built on sand is no more stable than the sand. Although thought and analysis abstract primary qualities from direct experience, it remains the case that the analysis rests on a supposedly subjective and unreliable basis. But if scientific results are sharable and repeatable, as seems to be the case, then their secondary-quality basis must in some sense be at least as reliable as are they.

More recently the term 'qualia' has been coined to denote secondary qualities such as a patch of yellow I now perceive, sometimes referred to as a 'sense datum'. The latter is now referred to as a 'quale', the singular of 'qualia'. However there is an ongoing debate among philosophers as to the status of qualia. Do they exist as a stratum of reality, or are they merely subjective illusions as science maintains? In other words, are the colours I experience as part of my environment an objective part of that environment or are they subjective constructs of my mental life added to it? It is paradoxical to say that qualia do not exist, for we all experience them. *Something* must correspond to them. How could I experience so vividly what does not exist? In any case, as already remarked, the objectivity of primary qualities rests—like it or not—on the basis of qualia. That is not to say, however, that *all* qualia are objective or that we may not be deceived by them on occasions. The shade of yellow I experience is after all affected by the environment and the state of my organism. But that does not make it non-existent. An interesting article on qualia may be consulted online in *Stanford Encyclopedia of Philosophy*.[7]

To approach this issue I will explore the role of the senses, and argue that they serve to make us conscious of our environment. Considering the eyes, we learn from physics that light enters the eye in the form of an image, leads to chemical changes in the retina, and then to nerve impulses that are transmitted to the brain after further processing in a little 'brain' behind the eyeball. The colour is no longer evident and some correspondence between brain states and the spectrum is only achieved much later after four levels of further processing. Something similar occurs for all the senses, including feelings. They all end up as nerve impulses processed by the brain, and then miraculously we become conscious of qualia at the end of all the processing. It has been argued that this disposes of qualia as part of the environment as all sense impressions are reduced to something similar, i.e. nerve impulses and the interaction between neurons in the brain. But that is not a necessary conclusion. If the role of the senses is to make us conscious of our environment, as I claim, then I do not expect them to 'convey' qualia as on a conveyer belt. Manifestly they do not. The complex processes of the brain in particular can instead be viewed as the means of making us conscious of what was sensed by the eyes, ears, etc. So it seems that a similar basic process for all the senses is involved to achieve that. Then instead of a 'miraculous process' at the end of the line, consciousness awakes in the totality of the process all the way from the object perceived to the final process in the brain. Thus the qualia are part of what is perceived. This conclusion lends support to its having a more objective status than hitherto supposed, lending credence to the common-sense view that my experience of a colour is qualitatively similar to yours, even if not identical. It follows that instead of a reductionist approach that leads to a dualism or parallelism between physical processes and qualia, there is a holistic process at work which we call 'consciousness', which achieves its result by means of the detailed processes involved. This is not necessarily intended to imply realism as opposed to idealism; I will return to that issue.

Now take the case of a colour-blind person. On the above analysis the conclusion is that the organism is defective so that consciousness of the correct colour cannot be evoked, but nevertheless some colour (in most cases) arises in consciousness. Similarly for the other senses. *That* a colour is being incorrectly or only partially rendered cannot be known from an analysis of perceptions alone, but only when thinking is brought to bear on the situation. Thus a knowledge of what is being perceived depends upon both perception and thinking. It is fruitless to attempt to base secure knowledge on an analysis of perception alone, for the role of thinking is indispensible.

This answers the charge of naive realism, for I am not accepting all qualia as objectively real. What I *am* doing is to say that they are indispensible to knowledge of myself and whatever world they subsist in, but cannot necessarily be taken at face value. A mirage, for example, exists *as a mirage* but not as an oasis. The great philosopher A.J. Ayer mistakenly thought that when I come to realize that I am only experiencing a mirage it is the senses that correct me.[8] No, it is my thinking that corrects me in the light of revised perceptions.

A further apparent objection is that I have naive-realistically accepted the structure and functioning of the eyes and brain, a mistake often made for example by Gonzalo Munevar.[9] But it should be clear from the above that such knowledge is based on a great deal of thinking and research, based indeed on qualia, but not in a naive sense.

These conclusions relate also to my feelings. Corresponding to various bodily processes feelings arise, but a feeling is itself a quale and thus to be regarded as such and not reduced to the action of brain cells or chemical processes. It has been maintained, particularly in the materialistic training of doctors of medicine, that feelings are merely chemical processes in the body. But chemical processes are just that. Only when seen as part of a process of arousing consciousness which entails qualia are those chemical processes seen in the right context. As far as love is concerned, I am (or may be) conscious of it but I do not find any external processes such as affect the senses to account for it. It is a purely inner experience, but not to be dismissed as illusion any more than is any other percept. Science deigns only to deal with externally observed processes, and does so very effectively. But it is missing half the reality, i.e. the inner aspects of existence, and so ends up with a quantum physics that is pure mathematics lacking any tangible content.

I have been careful in the above discussion to try to avoid dualism. My reason for that is that dualism posits two kinds of reality that cannot be reduced to each other or even reconciled. Descartes famously foundered on the apparent duality between mind and body, being unable to see how the one acted upon the other.[10] Bertrand Russell and Karl Popper are examples of philosophers who were dualistic in that they accepted the existence of a Platonic world of ideas distinct from the world of experience, but found no bridge between the two. It is hardly satisfactory to resort to opposites that are unable to affect each other and yet seem to do so in practice. There may appear to be a dualism between my perceptions (qualia) and the concepts I arrive at through thinking, but that is more apparent than real as will be seen.

I have arrived at a point where I accept as a genuine part of the world my experiences as given by my perceptions and feelings and made conscious with the help of the senses and the brain. But also I refrain from accepting the results naively for it is clear that all experience needs to be evaluated before its true status is known. I do not yet know whether it is all a kind of semblance backed by a transcendental reality, or purely in our minds although of significance, or is actual reality. Thus I must now turn to the conceptual side of my knowledge.

Concepts

I have many concepts that make my life intelligible, such as: man, cat, house, leaf, cause-and-effect, colour, sound, and so on. Suppose you have never seen a cat before, and one enters the room. The experience leaves you with a memory picture which you can recall, so you have inwardly changed slightly as you now possess a new picture. On seeing that cat again you recognize it thanks to that picture, and learn that the creature is called a 'cat'. On seeing a second cat of a different colour you recognize its shape and behaviour but nevertheless see that it is not quite the same. After seeing several different cats something magic happens: you have a new concept that embraces all the prior memory pictures. The magic is that any cat is now recognizable. You have changed inwardly more radically in now possessing a new concept that has a potentially infinite domain, i.e. all possible cats—past, present and near future. The jump from memory of a few instances to embracing an infinitude of possible cases is when the concept is formed. It is thinking that makes that jump and forges the new concept, for concepts are thought, not perceived. This is not analytical thinking, but another kind that grasps commonality rather than distinction. It may subsequently happen that for the first time you see a Manx cat with no tail. Thinking then recognizes it as a cat and simultaneously extends the concept to include cats with no tail. That is a remarkable process, all too easily overlooked, because flexibility is combined with recognition. I know a cat when I see one because I unite my concept with the perception. My knowledge in a practical sense is *my ability to unite appropriate concepts with percepts*, a process carried out by my thinking, although I am not usually conscious of that thinking. This is a species of the performance theory of knowledge, for I can perform in a certain sense when I have concepts and can think. But it is not such as to reduce everything to mere action devoid of inner content.

An error of judgement, philosophically speaking, is to unite an inappropriate concept with a perception. Thus I see a lake down in the valley and judge it to be oval. When I reach the lake I find that after all it is circular. The error lay neither in the initial perception (perceptions cannot be 'wrong') nor in the concept 'oval' (concepts cannot be 'wrong' either) but in my false judgement that the lake was oval. It is of course possible to form concepts that have no domain of application, e.g. pink elephants, but even such a concept is not 'wrong' but useless. Such a concept is not meaningless as contended by the positivists, for I can well attach a meaning to 'pink elephant' and would recognize one were I to meet it. The danger lies in clinging to concepts that have no domain of application.

How secure is our knowledge, when viewed as the ability to unite appropriate concepts with percepts? For scepticism maintains it is not possible to have any certain knowledge. My answer is that my conceptual base gives me secure knowledge *within its valid domain*. Returning to my ability to recognize cats, my concept prior to seeing a Manx cat was not useless because it omitted Manx cats; on the contrary it was very useful, but unknown to me its domain was restricted. On seeing the Manx cat that defect was repaired, but without throwing all previous experience in the rubbish bin. My knowledge was extended rather than contradicted. A philosophy of science seeks a definition that includes recognized scientific disciplines while rejecting others. The various solutions offered tend to concentrate on whether theories are scientific. Consider the concept of gravity. It was first recognized and described by Sir Isaac Newton. His theory is still widely used as it is very useful and appears to be accurate within its domain. Albert Einstein proposed a quite different theory, but its domain coincides with Newton's for most practical purposes, including the launching of space probes, but handles extreme cases such as black holes where Newton's does not. The progress was to extend the domain of the concept to special extreme cases. But never did the concept become 'wrong'. Indeed omitting the mathematics it has hardly changed as it is the concept that massive objects tend to approach each other, which is common to both versions. Thus well-tested concepts give us secure knowledge, but we remain open to them being refined and extended as science progresses. The sceptic is wrong in saying we have no secure knowledge. He is only right if we insist that what we have is the last word. Were he absolutely right it is hard to see how everyday life could proceed as successfully as it does, for our daily activity continuously involves applying concepts to attain our ends. My wife definitely knows how to cook a good meal! A good example of a concept that grows is that of my wife. I think I know her, but as life goes on and new situations are met she can surprise me even after many years! But that does not mean I knew nothing of her before.

Now the processes in the world that I know about continue regardless of my personal knowledge, so what I have grasped as concept is also part of those processes. Gravity acts remorselessly and mere perceptions of bodies falling down is only half the story. The conceptual aspect of my knowledge is active in the behaviour of falling bodies, as is readily testable. In this sense our concepts are also part of the world, and it is more accurate to suppose that in the concept I have grasped an aspect of the world not accessible to bare perception. It is as though I have 'observed' that aspect through thinking about my perceptions. That 'observation' process may be called *intuition* to distinguish it from the customary use of the word 'observation'. Through intuition I unite with what I perceive and grasp its conceptual aspect. Thus my knowledge is to a small degree participatory, although that is not readily apparent. Of course the words I use to denote concepts are part of me (I won't see 'gravity' written on a falling body!) but the non-verbal aspect of the concept, which is what is important, is what is shared with the world. Thus I am part of the world not only through breathing and eating but also in my life of concepts. That is normally outside my consciousness, however, which is why it is non-verbal. It is also why the continuous process of recognizing objects around me is not accompanied by conscious sentences such as 'that is a cat'. This is better illustrated by tacit knowledge. For example, I know how to ride a bicycle, but the concepts of balance and how to achieve it, etc. involved in that knowledge are quite unconscious.

A centuries-old debate concerned whether concepts are part of the world we live in ('realism' in its old sense) or are only labels in men's heads ('nominalism'). The latter contended that my concepts are only in me, so that the concept 'cat' is only a word that I have learnt how to use. Let us return to the cat! When a cat enters the room I recognize it immediately. However I do not fish about wondering which label to attach ('dog', 'parrot', 'cat' . . .) but rather I recognize it and then know what to call it. I only know which 'label' to attach *after* I have recognized it, in which case the label merely serves the purpose of communication with others. Yet the concept enables me to recognize it. A mere label could never achieve that. That is because the concept is not merely in me but is also in the cat (see the previous paragraph). I arrive at a position that is reminiscent of Platonism in that what is usually regarded as an ideal content (concepts and universals) is seen to exist independently of me but differs in that, rather than supposing there is another Platonic world distinct from that of experience, I regard that ideal content as belonging to the world of experience— which is perhaps more Aristotelian.

One practical hint. To grasp a new concept, which can be difficult, it is helpful to have several examples where it applies which are as different as possible apart from that concept. An example of this will arise below for thinking.

I now require both concepts and perceptions to arrive at useful if restricted knowledge, but the significant essence of concepts lies in the non-verbal realm and so their credentials, for all their usefulness, needs clarification.

The Role of Thinking

It is a plain fact of observation that I think. For example, if I observe that the ceiling is damp I immediately respond inwardly with the question 'what caused that?' and then go further by suspecting a tile on the roof is loose. This inner activity is added to mere observation. I observe that this inner process becomes active, and soon realize that it is going on most of my waking life. If I have to construct a picture (cf. the need to form a picture of how to act), I am aware of a quite strenuous inner activity attempting to do so. If I want to work out how much three kilos of carrots will cost and have forgotten to bring my calculator, I engage in some mental arithmetic. If I have to plan a party next week, I try to envisage how much food and drink are required for the number of guests involved, what activities to lay on and so forth, and then how to obtain what is needed. Another example already encountered was the activity that arrives at a new concept. In each of the above examples I am aware of being inwardly active. That inner activity I call 'thinking'. So thinking is not 'mere calculation' as is sometimes supposed, but an inner process that includes calculation; it is also an organizing activity, a picture building process, the welding of separate experiences into concepts. The *technique* in each case is different, but the inner drive is similar. The concept 'thinking' emerges from the experience of all these types of activity, as well as others not mentioned. Far from being a vague concept, as has been claimed academically, thinking is a definite process that takes place in the different examples of thought activity, which can be experienced but not easily defined. There can be a fear in some thinkers of accepting as a result that a non-physical activity is present in us.

It is very often maintained that thinking is only a brain activity, i.e. that the brain does the thinking. But that is an unproved theory. Indeed thinking is needed to frame that theory, so thinking comes first—whatever it may turn out to be. No explanation has been found to date as to how thoughts and concepts are created by the brain. That I need my brain is clear, but its role needs clarification. I need a spade to dig the garden, but the spade does not do the digging; I dig *with* the spade. Likewise thinking needs the brain but it is not logically necessarily that it is done by the brain. It has been shown that complex brain activity is involved in becoming conscious of qualia, and since the same kind of activity is active when I am thinking (i.e. complex interactions of neurons via nerve impulses accompanied by chemical activity) it is reasonable to suppose that thinking uses the brain to make the results of its activity conscious. A consistent approach, then, is to regard the brain as an organ used both by perception and thinking to become conscious. None of the remarkable discoveries of the workings of the brain in the past decades is contradicted or devalued by this approach. I regard those processes as a part of consciousness-raising, which points to the complexity of consciousness itself. Thinking, as I observe, is an inner activity along with other inner activities, although it differs significantly in that I have to be proactive for it to occur. In contrast as soon as I am awake perceptions bombard me without any need for me to take initiative. Creative thinking requires consciously attempted inner activity and initiative. Thus perceptions are largely given—indeed imposed—while concepts arrived at through thinking must be worked for.

Just as we are not conscious of light itself but of objects illuminated by it, so we are not usually conscious of thinking itself but of what we are thinking about. Julian Jaynes[11] pointed out that we are not conscious of thinking. But it is possible to become conscious of thinking, *by thinking about it* (as a process). It is the one process that can be applied to itself.[12] When I try this, at first I find 'gaps', i.e. I see that I moved from one thought to another but the transition is not clear. Like moving my arm, I see *that* it happened but not how. But gradually with practice I find my consciousness becoming enhanced so that I wake up as it were in the gaps. I can then awake to a higher mode of thinking and consciousness to which I will return.

Through observing and thinking about thinking I arrive at a concept of it which *it* has produced. I cannot doubt the validity of this for to know anything consciously I must think, and here I am immersed first hand in the production of a concept by means of thinking which is independent of sense perception. I know that thinking is a self-validating process as it can study and evaluate itself. Indeed we do this evaluation constantly when we test conclusions arrived at by thinking. Science supposes thinking is tested by observation and must be so tested. However that is only a partial description, for it is thinking that uses observation to test its own conclusions. Deny the validity of thinking and those very tests are invalidated. So I have in thinking the one process that can give me reliable knowledge and which is in itself free of external factors that might otherwise throw doubt on its independence. Thus the concepts arrived at through it are also underwritten by it. Hence my knowledge is secured as far as concepts are concerned, and also the role of perception is underwritten by thinking which evaluates it too. Theories on the other hand go beyond concepts and percepts and are not as secure. They relate several concepts in a hypothetical manner. How many have been discarded! The philosophy of science has become utilitarian as truth seems beyond the reach of science, e.g. Sir Karl Popper[13] who believed in truth—unlike others—but paradoxically evolved a philosophy unable to reach it. He regarded all science as 'instrumental', i.e. practically useful but not yielding truth.

Love as a concept is gained from my experience as well as from the observation of others, and shares the security of concepts described above.

But what is the nature of thinking and other inner experiences?

What are Inner Experiences?

Qualia, consciousness and thinking have been discussed above without regard to their nature. Are they physical? Or are they emergent entities? Or do they belong to another category or kind of existence? Can they be reduced to properties of the physical world, or are they distinct? The reason the term 'qualia' is useful is that qualities are taken seriously. However, 'quality' is often emergent. Thus to say my shoes are of good quality does not mean that quality is an added ingredient: it is emergent, meaning that thanks to good materials and workmanship my shoes are of good quality. Now a colour such as yellow as a quality of an object is regarded by physics in just this way: there is not supposed to be any 'added ingredient', instead the radiation reflected by the object has wavelengths whose aggregate causes me to experience yellow. So the quality-problem is solved for the physical world by denying it exists there, at the expense of an unclear, unsolved notion that my organism is in some unknown way responsible for it. The logic is completed by physics washing its hands of the problem by refusing to admit that secondary qualities are part of its remit. However the introduction of qualia by philosophers as 'added ingredients' instead of emergent properties enables that unsatisfactory situation to be tackled. But ingredients are, to put it crudely, 'made of something'. Just as flour, butter, milk, etc. are distinct ingredients that make up a cake, so qualia are distinct ingredients of reality. But what is the nature of those ingredients? Aristotle proposed ten 'categories' one of which is substance, quality being a distinct category. Physics sees substance as 'real' and physical, and all other categories including quality as emergent. It recognizes the existence of fields such as electric fields but reduces them to the exchange of subtle particles which are in turn 'physical' in some sense. The paradox physics ends up with is that its foundation is quantum physics which is purely mathematical, substance being an emergent property that is not explained clearly.

The reason some philosophers vehemently reject the real existence of qualia is that they are afraid of adding another kind of 'ingredient' of reality that is not physical and raises the spectre (for them) of souls, spirits and goodness knows what else. They prefer 'physicalism' which holds that all aspects of reality are reducible to physical processes. By accepting the existence of qualia I also accept the existence of more than one ingredient of reality. But now the spectre not just of dualism but pluralism arises. Is a 'layer-cake' model implied where the lowest layer of reality is physical, other layers being added by the various types of qualia? Or is an 'ingredient' model more appropriate where each kind of quality—

including the physical—is an ingredient of reality? That returns us to Aristotle, for then his substance is not to be identified with the physical, but is what contains, or is made of, all the ingredients. Materialism is then left behind as substance is not merely material in the way science imagines, but is much richer.

The conclusion to be drawn from either model is that feeling, thinking, consciousness and all inward qualities—together with the physical—are distinct ingredients that are not reducible to each other. In particular they are not reducible to the physical. I prefer the ingredient model to the layer-cake one as the latter inherits the well-known problems exemplified by dualism, whereas in the ingredient model the ingredients interact via the substance of which they are a part. Physicalism is thus also rejected by this approach. Left open is the most interesting question: what is the nature of the ground substance as it is not exclusively physical/material?

It may appear that realism (in its modern sense) has been adopted above. Realism says that there is a real world 'out there' that is independent of human (or other) consciousness. There are broadly two versions: that reality is material/physical, or that it is spiritual. Idealism or anti-realism, in contrast, sees all phenomena as states or modifications of our mental life. A stone is not 'out there made of substance' but is a phenomenon of consciousness. Bishop Berkeley[14] famously wrote that *'esse est percipi'*: to exist is to be perceived. A tree exists because I perceive it. Then as a good bishop he solved the problem of whether it continues to exist when no one is perceiving it by saying that God perceives it! So far philosophers have been unable to reach agreement as to whether realism or idealism is correct. The ingredient model I propose seems to imply realism. That is not a necessary conclusion, however, as the nature of substance has not been clarified. Perhaps it is ideal? I used the term 'real' not in the sense of realism, but as what for us is significant in everyday life. Idealism does not say our experience is unreal, but rather says reality is not independent of perception. A problem is, however, that we do not perceive substance directly, but its ingredients, so Berkeley's version of idealism becomes rather strained. For the moment I accept realism in the spiritual sense, i.e. that there is a real world of which I am a part, the ground of reality being spiritual. Physics has been driven very close to that view with its essentially mathematical basis that involves continuous action but finds substance hard to define. Of course it does not wish to make the final step of recognizing the action as spiritual, but then what is 'action'? Some kind of agent must act. That leads us to the whole question of spirituality.

Spiritual Activity

Earlier I described how thinking may be applied to itself. Thinking is not based on sense perception, for thinking has no colour, size, taste or other sense-perceptible qualities! So what is the content of my thinking when I am thinking about thinking? Evidently it is non-sense-perceptible. It is an activity that we may call 'spiritual' as it cannot be reduced to the physical. We may wake up to it in the 'gaps' described earlier. To many this will seem rather a thin concept of the spirit, but that shows they have not experienced it. In any case it is only a beginning. Some people are gifted with rich spiritual experience, but a gift has not been acquired consciously (at least in this life). Thinking about thinking can be done by anyone, not merely the specially gifted, and so is a bridge open to everyone leading from ordinary consciousness to a higher one, and open to richer development.

Thinking is thus a spiritual activity which is the ground of certain knowledge as it is self-supporting and thus needs no justification outside itself. As a thinker I am, then, a spiritual being. But there is more to it than that. Throughout this essay I have used thinking to discuss the world we live in, our own constitution and the existence of freedom. How can we be sure that thinking is applicable to the questions raised, and to unravelling the riddle of the world in general? It might be supposed that it is a subjective activity that only reveals my subjective self and its efforts to attain knowledge. What, however, distinguishes between 'objective' and 'subjective'? Those concepts are derived by thinking! But that implies thinking itself transcends the distinction. Were thinking subjective then that distinction would exist before thinking made it, which contradicts the fact that thinking made it. Also, the distinction could not be made other than by thinking, as it can exist only as a thought-construct, i.e. it can have no other kind of existence (e.g. as a material body). There are no purple objects running around which are the distinction between subject and object! It might be objected that the distinction was made by some other thinking agent—since it must be made by thinking— and our thinking arose afterwards *within* the distinction. That is indeed possible, but it only reinforces the point I am making, that some level of thinking supersedes the distinction. That we are able to discuss the whole issue in this way shows that *our* thinking partakes of that level. Then thinking is not in fact itself subjective if it transcends that concept, in which case it bridges the subjective and the objective and so I conclude that I may safely apply it to the world. *Thinking bridges the subjective and the objective.* The other point to note about thinking

43

in this respect is that to obtain conscious knowledge we have no choice but to employ it! To say thinking is of no value is self-contradictory as that very statement is based on thinking. This is not an unfreedom, however, any more than I am unfree because I need a screwdriver to tighten a screw. I would be unfree if could *not* use my thinking.

If, then, thinking transcends my subjectivity then it does so for other people too. We all share something in that we think. That is why we can share the results of thinking in principle with full clarity, e.g. mathematics. Feeling on the other hand is notoriously hard to share in the same way, while wills clash more readily than they cooperate. What is the bearer of this common life of thinking? Because my subjectivity is transcended that bearer is also transcendent, which leads to the conclusion that we all participate in a common higher spiritual life of which we are the branches. Is my individuality an illusion, then? If not, then that higher spiritual life must be the ground of individuality and the bearer of individualities. Undoubtedly it must be of a much higher stature than me, involving the love in thinking necessary to embrace us all. Different religions give different names to this higher spiritual life, but I do not wish to give it a name as the point here is to recognize its existence without recourse to dogma or faith. Then it may enable us to transcend the differences between religions precisely because their ultimate foundation is common, even if decked out in their differing fancy clothes, which are not what is essential.

Summary and Conclusion

Free deeds involve love in its three main forms: love in thinking, love in feeling and love in the will. Love is not a scientific concept and cannot be compelled, and thus guarantees the freedom of actions based upon it. Freedom is beyond the reach of science, to be taken hold of gradually by human beings. It shares with other inner experiences *that* reality grasped by thinking about experiences which is made conscious in concepts. Thinking itself is a self-supporting spiritual activity that is indispensible and self-correcting. It is also the bridge between the subjective and the objective, leading to the recognition of a higher spirituality grounded in love that is shared by all human beings the world over.

Thus knowledge is secure within the domain of our conceptual base, while freedom is a possibility to be grasped, which is possible.

Annex A

Science and Freedom

Benjamin Libet[15] demonstrated that preparatory activity in the organism begins a fraction of a second before a person is conscious of making the resolve to act, and concluded that the body 'decides' to act and freedom is an illusion because consciousness does not come first. More recently work done using fMRI has substantiated Libet's findings[16]. The laboratory conditions leading to that conclusion are extrapolated to all human action. But what is omitted is an understanding of the nature of human will. It is surely obvious that we are unconscious in our will. I am not conscious of the many processes that enable me to move my hand, for example. All I am conscious of is my thought that I must reach out, and then the fact that I do so. The way thought is translated into action is quite unclear to me. I am referring here to the actual will rather than its bodily manifestations, as for example in the 'will to live' manifest by some critically ill people.

As long as I remain unconscious in my will, my freedom lies in my conscious thinking, and that of the will vicariously lies in its relation to thinking. So freedom cannot without further ado be ascribed to the will. But the given relationship between thinking and will provides an interim stage whereby we are partially free as a whole, i.e. as thinking, feeling and willing beings. Full freedom not only in thinking but also of the will requires consciousness of the will itself, which is attainable by spiritual development. Libet's experiment does no more than demonstrate that normally we are unconscious in our will. The freedom of his volunteers lay in agreeing to do the experiment.

It could be said that Libet's argument applies to that very agreement, but agreement is certainly only achieved after conscious thought, so any action potential prior to that must refer not to the agreement but to preparing to hear the proposal.

Finally, love is not a scientific factor and so is necessarily absent from any acceptably arranged scientific experiment, which on my thesis renders the experiment sterile from the outset.

Annex B

Meaning

Something has meaning to me if I care about it, otherwise not. To care involves love to some degree. A relationship has meaning if it enhances the quality of my life and that of the other. Also, of course, if it proves a hindrance that challenges me. Accepting a challenge involves love in the will. Improved quality of life is perceived as such because it contains an element I love. A blow of fate has meaning in the first sense, but at a deeper level if for me it accomplishes something important. Something is important to me if I value it, and valuing involves feeling. That feeling in turn involves love for what is felt to be important. Perhaps through the event I gain greater insight into myself or into others, or into life itself. Perhaps I am strengthened in the long term even though initially I feel abused. Perhaps I overcome a character defect through it, or develop a new ability I previously lacked. Without love such things are meaningless. To go into denial is precisely *not* to love what has happened and to wish it had not. Take away love and events become happenings lacking any human significance. Hatred involves meaning in the roundabout manner that it implies the opposite of something I love. Why hate otherwise? I do not wish to advocate an exclusively supernaturalistic, naturalistic, subjectivist or objectivist view here, for love can be involved in all those views, even if a bit strained for the objectivists.

Even the meaning of sentences involves feeling. First it is clear that marks on a piece of paper are no more than that until read by a human being. There is no meaning without human involvement, which also is certainly true of what I hear. A sentence has meaning if I feel it does! This is rather obvious and flies in the face of a more academic view. 'Two plus two equals four', 'The present Queen of France has red hair', 'Pink elephants like pomegranates' all have meaning, which should not be confused with whether or not they are true. 'Fackleboms bo henderdracks' has no meaning (at least to me!) because I cannot feel what it asserts, much less explain it. Feeling is a perception, i.e. *meaning is perceived*. I can perceive the meaning of the first three propositions, but not the fourth. But what I perceive lies not in the sentence itself but in what I make of it. Sentences are only such for human beings. First I have to be able to think it, and then to perceive meaning in the thought, or not. Here feeling is a perception that what initially is in me, as a result of thinking the sentence, has significance beyond mere me. I perceive my relation to what the sentence is about. Only if I feel such a relation do I perceive meaning in the sentence.

Formal meaning boils down to whether a sentence

makes sense, which again turns on whether I can perceive its reference.

I should perhaps stress that I am using 'feeling' above in its more objective sense as a species of perception in contrast to subjective likes, dislikes and prejudices.

Thus meaning involves feeling as a perception, and in the case of life that involves love.

References

1. Alfred North Whitehead, *Science and the Modern World* (1925), Cambridge University Press, 2011

2. Rudolf Steiner, *Die Philosophie der Freiheit* (1894, revised edition 1918). English editions include *The Philosophy of Freedom*, translated by Michael Wilson, RSP, 1964, 1999. There are also translations with the alternative title *The Philosophy of Spiritual Activity*

3. George (Bishop) Berkeley, *Principles of Human Knowledge* (1710)

4. Rudolf Steiner, lecture 16 in *Man Hieroglyph of the Universe*, RSP 1972

5. Galileo, *Il Saggiatore* (*The Assayer*) (1623)

6. Thomas Hobbes, e.g. *The Elements of Law* (1640)

7. *Stanford Encyclopedia of Philosophy*, online at http://plato.stanford.edu/entries/qualia

8. A.J. Ayer, *Language, Truth and Logic*, Victor Gollancz, London 1936; Penguin, 2001

9. Gonzalo Munevar, *Radical Knowledge*, Avebury Publishing Company, 1981

10. René Descartes, *Principia Philosophiae* (*Principles of Philosophy*) (1644)

11. Julian Jaynes, *The Origin of Consciousness in the Breakdown of the Bicameral Mind* (1976), Penguin Books, 1993

12. Steiner, *The Philosophy of Freedom*

13. Karl R. Popper, *Conjectures and Refutations: Growth of Scientific Knowledge*, Routledge & Kegan Paul, London 1963, 2002

14. Berkeley, *Principles of Human Knowledge*
15. Benjamin Libet, 'Unconscious cerebral initiative and the role of conscious will in voluntary action', in *Behavioral and Brain Sciences*, vol. 8, issue 04, December 1985
16. Bode, He, Soon, Trampel, Turner & Haynes, 'Tracking the unconscious generation of free decisions using ultra-high field fMRI', Public Library of Science, 6 (6) e21612